spot

BACKYARD ANIMALS

MICE

by Marysa Storm

AMICUS | AMICUS INK

tail

ears

Look for these
words and pictures
as you read.

nose

nails

What's on that branch?
It's a mouse!

Mice are rodents.
They can live anywhere.
They can even live
in Antarctica!

Look at the mouse's tail.
It is long and thin.
It can be as long as
a mouse's body!

tail

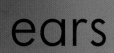

ears

Look at the mouse's large ears.
Mice have excellent hearing.

Look at the mouse's pointed nose.
Mice have a good sense of smell.

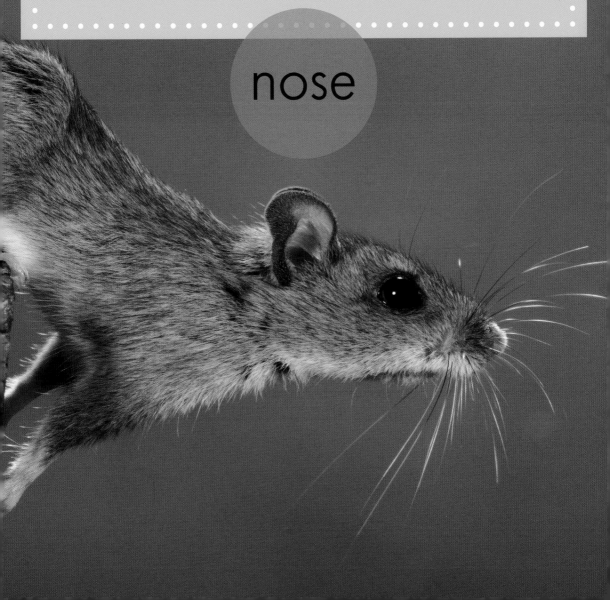

nose

nails

Look at the mouse's feet.
They have sharp nails.
These help the mouse climb.

Mice go out at night.
This mouse is looking for dinner.
Seeds! Yum!

tail

ears

nose

Did you find?

nails

Spot is published by Amicus and Amicus Ink
P.O. Box 1329, Mankato, MN 56002
www.amicuspublishing.us

Library of Congress Cataloging-in-Publication Data
Names: Storm, Marysa, author.
Title: Mice / by Marysa Storm.
Description: Mankato, Minnesota : Amicus, [2018] | Series:
  Spot. Backyard animals | Audience: Grade K-3.
Identifiers: LCCN 2016044421 (print) | LCCN 2017000793
  (ebook) | ISBN 9781681510934 (library binding) | ISBN
  9781681511832 (e-book) | ISBN 9781681522180 (pbk.)
Subjects: LCSH: Mice--Juvenile literature.
Classification: LCC QL737.R6 S713 2018 (print) | LCC
  QL737.R6 (ebook) | DDC 599.35/3--dc23
LC record available at https://lccn.loc.gov/2016044421

Printed in the United States of America

HC  10 9 8 7 6 5 4 3 2 1
PB  10 9 8 7 6 5 4 3 2 1

Rebecca Glaser, editor
Deb Miner, series designer
Ciara Beitlich, book designer
Holly Young, photo researcher

Photos by 123RF 1, 2, 8–9, 15;
Alamy/Louise Heusinkveld 3,
Andrew Darrington 2, 10–11, 15,
TomsPhotos 2, 12–13, 15; Getty/Dr
T J Martin 14; iStock cover 2, 6–7,
15; Shutterstock 4–5

MICE